NORTHERN PROVINCE
RIVONIA
JOHANNESBURG
SHARPEVILLE
FORTHARE
KRUGER
GAUTENG
MBASHE RIVER
FREE STATE
KWAZULU NATAL
LESOTHO
MVEZO
UMTATA
FORT HARE
SOUTH AFRICA

For my son, James Redden McDonough,
whose future holds such promise.
—Y. Z. M.

For Mimi Vang Olsen, my dear friend, and Tim Travaglini, my editor.
—M. Z.

Text copyright © 2002 by Yona Zeldis McDonough
Illustrations copyright © 2002 by Malcah Zeldis

First published in the United States of America in 2002 by
Walker Publishing Company, Inc.

Published simultaneously in Canada by Fitzhenry and Whiteside, Markham, Ontario L3R 4T8

For information about permission to reproduce selections from this book,
write to Permissions, Walker & Company, 435 Hudson Street, New York, New York 10014

Library of Congress Cataloging-in-Publication Data

McDonough, Yona Zeldis.
Peaceful protest : the life of Nelson Mandela/Yona Zeldis McDonough;
illustrations by Malcah Zeldis.
p. cm.
Summary: A biography of the black South African leader who became a
civil rights activist, political prisoner, and president of South Africa.
ISBN 0-8027-8821-1—ISBN 0-8027-8823-8
1. Mandela, Nelson, 1918–Juvenile literature. 2. Presidents—South Africa—Biography—Juvenile literature.
[1. Mandela, Nelson, 1918- 2. Presidents—South Africa. 3. Civil rights workers. 4. Nobel Prizes—Biography.
5. Blacks—South Africa—Biography.] I. Zeldis, Malcah, ill. II. Title.
DT1974 .M38 2002
968.06'5'092—dc21
2002023462

Book design by Claire Counihan

Printed in Hong Kong

2 4 6 8 10 9 7 5 3 1

The artist used gouache on watercolor paper
to create the illustrations for this book.

Visit Walker & Company's Web site at www.walkerbooks.com

(B)

PEACEFUL PROTEST

The Life of Nelson Mandela

Yona Zeldis McDonough

Illustrations by Malcah Zeldis

Walker & Company
New York

Buti Mandela was born July 18, 1918,

in the South African village of Mvezo. His father, Chief Gadla Hendry Mphakanyiswa, of the Mandela family, was a wise and respected ruler of the Thembu people.

The Thembu, whose ancestors had lived in Africa for many years, were dark skinned. But although Africa was their country, they were always at the mercy of the white settlers—mostly English, but also Dutch—who had invaded their land in the 1700s and who continued to control and dominate them.

Once, when Chief Hendry was summoned by the English magistrate over a complaint about an ox, he refused to appear before the white man. In his mind, a Thembu chief was only bound to obey the Thembu king, not an English official. As a result of his defiance, Hendry was forced to give up his role as chief. Because of his beliefs, he lost his land, his cattle, and his respected position.

Although Buti was just a baby when this happened, he grew up knowing that his father was a man who stood firm in his convictions, even when those convictions had a high price.

The family moved to the nearby village of Qunu, where they lived on the *kraal*—or farm—of their relatives. Although Qunu was a humble place, Buti liked it. His house consisted of three grass-roofed huts, the walls of which had been made from mud molded into bricks. One hut was for cooking, one was for sleeping, and one was for storing food. The chairs were made from mud, and the stove was little more than a hole in the ground.

During the day, Buti herded the cattle and played in the fields with his friends and half brothers and sisters. His father, according to African custom, had four wives and a total of thirteen children. The boys made their own toys, using clay to shape animals and birds; they played *ndize* (hide and seek), *icekwa* (touch and run), and *thinti* (a childish version of war).

At night, Buti lay down to sleep on a mat. His parents told marvelous bedtime stories: His father's were about heroic warriors and battles; his mother's were legends and fables that the Thembu people had told for generations.

When Buti was seven years old, his parents were encouraged to send him to school. Even though Hendry Mandela had not gone to school himself, he decided that his son ought to have the chance. Buti's three half brothers had already grown up and left home. So Buti became the first person in his family to attend school.

On the first day, the teacher gave all the children English names. Buti came home and told his family to call him Nelson, the new name the teacher had given him. Since the school was run by British settlers, the students were taught that British ways—language, history, beliefs, and culture—were superior. They were not taught to value the traditions and customs of their own people.

Yet Nelson liked school. There were new things to discover every day, and he was given a small slate board with sticks of chalk to write the many things he learned.

In 1927, when Nelson was nine years old, his father died. He mourned the man who had set such a powerful example of standing up for what he believed to be right.

Hendry Mandela's dying wish was for his son Nelson to receive a good education and become the kind of man who set an example to his people. So Nelson and his mother left Qunu and the village school he had outgrown. They set out on foot for Mqekezweni, the capital of Thembuland. He arrived carrying a tin trunk and wearing an old shirt, shorts that had been cut down from his father's pants, and a belt made of rope. Mqekezweni was called "The Great Place" by the Africans who lived in the region, and Nelson was astounded by its motorcars, grand houses, beautiful gardens, and orchards filled with peach and apple trees.

Nelson lived with a relative of his father's, Chief Jongintaba Dalindyebo, who had agreed to be his guardian. Soon the shy village boy grew accustomed to his new life. The chief's children and Nelson all became close, attending school and church together. Nelson did well in school, although he later said that it was not because he was so clever but rather because he had a fierce desire to succeed.

One of the things Nelson liked best about life in The Great Place was the chance to see all the important visitors who gathered at Mqekezweni to seek the advice and guidance of Chief Dalindyebo. It was from these men that Nelson learned about African history and the great heroes of the past. The stories they told stayed with him for a long time.

At sixteen, Nelson was ready to participate in the ritual passage into manhood. For the boys of his tribe, this meant traveling to the banks of the Mbashe River. With the village elders to guide them, the boys rubbed white clay all over their bodies and put on grass skirts. They danced and told stories. One of the speakers made a deep impression on Nelson. He told all the boys that their promise of manhood would remain unfulfilled, because all black South Africans were a conquered people—slaves in their own land, denied their freedoms and their rights.

Many years later Nelson wrote about the effect of hearing those words as a young man. He said that although he was not ready to act on them at the time, the ideas stayed with him, shaping his vision of the world and his place in it.

Nelson continued his education, first at Clarkebury Boarding Institute, a Thembu college in the district of Engcobo, and then at Fort Hare, a school in the municipality of Alice run by British missionaries for black students from all over Africa. At Fort Hare, he began to shed some of his country ways: He learned to use a toothbrush and toothpaste, instead of ash to whiten his teeth and toothpicks to clean them. Wearing pajamas, using flush toilets, and taking hot-water showers were also novelties to him.

He studied hard and was a good student, although he still found time to join the track team and learn ballroom dancing. During his last year at Fort Hare, Nelson was elected to serve on the student council. But in 1940, after a disagreement with the head of the school, he left Fort Hare before graduating.

Back at The Great Place, Nelson had a surprise. His guardian, Chief Dalindyebo, had arranged a marriage for him, and for his "brother," the Chief's son, Justice. Although arranging marriages was a traditional African custom, Nelson and Justice had other ideas. Together, they ran away to the big city of Johannesburg. Nelson had dreams of becoming a lawyer and was able to get work with a sympathetic white lawyer named Lazar Sidelsky. While training at Sidelsky's office, Nelson was able to continue his education.

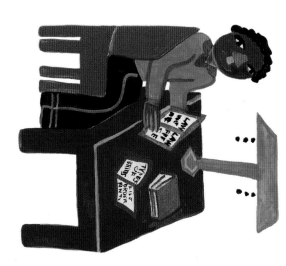

Life in Johannesburg gave Nelson another kind of education. To a boy from the country, the city was a rough, confusing, and crowded place. And it was in Johannesburg that Nelson saw how badly blacks were treated by the whites who held power: Forced into restricted living areas, their homes were poor and cramped, lacking electricity, plumbing, and heat. They were forced to ride "African only" buses, and eat in "African only" restaurants.

But perhaps even worse was the passbook: When a black man left the area to work elsewhere in the city, he had to carry a small passbook. Without a valid passbook, he could be thrown in jail.

The South African government had a name for these practices: *apartheid*, meaning "apart." In the United States, similar policies existed and were known as "segregation." Under apartheid, it was illegal for blacks and whites to eat, shop, travel, live, or attend school or church together. Nelson saw all of these things, and slowly there grew in him a desire to change them.

Despite all the odds against him, Nelson prospered in Johannesburg. He held a good job and continued his studies. He met Evelyn Mase, the cousin of a friend; the two fell in love and married.

Together they had two sons, Thembekile and Makgatho, and a daughter named Makaziwe.

Nelson began attending meetings where people shared his outrage over the unfair treatment of blacks. These people—some black and some white—called themselves the African National Congress, or ANC.

Together, they vowed to change the racist laws that condemned black people to live in poverty, ignorance, and fear. While some members of the ANC viewed the whites in their country as the enemy, Nelson had a more moderate view: He believed that whites and other racial groups should remain in South Africa, but that white supremacy had to end.

Nelson fulfilled his dream and became a lawyer. He and a partner, Oliver Tambo, opened the first black law practice in the city of Johannesburg in 1953. As Nelson's involvement with politics grew, his marriage to Evelyn suffered and eventually she left him. After their divorce, Nelson was introduced to a beautiful and lively young social worker named Winifred Nomzamo Madikizela. They soon fell in love and married. Together, they had two daughters, Zeni and Zindzi.

Nelson began organizing protest marches, boycotts, and strikes. He wrote articles for a journal called *Liberation* and became involved with another magazine called *Fighting Talk.* In these ways, he hoped to encourage people to join the struggle for equality.

Nelson saw that the issue of the passbooks was becoming more and more critical. Every year, hundreds of thousands of South African blacks were detained and convicted for failing to have the proper passbooks. Sometimes people were arrested while standing a few feet in front of their own houses, with their passbooks just inside.

In 1960 another of the anti-apartheid leaders organized a protest. He told the blacks to intentionally leave their passbooks at home and offer themselves for arrest. In the town of Sharpeville (near the city of Johannesburg) nearly fifteen thousand people gathered—without their passbooks—in front of the Sharpeville police station. The police opened fire on these unarmed men and women, killing sixty-nine people and wounding nearly two hundred more. To show his support, Nelson publicly burned his own passbook.

Soon people began to hear about Nelson Mandela; many of the whites who did grew both afraid and angry. They didn't like what Nelson was doing. They wanted the blacks to remain under their control. They wanted things in South Africa to remain the way they were.

One night while Nelson was asleep in bed, his door was kicked in violently by four policemen and he was dragged off to jail. Nelson was jailed many times for his anti-apartheid beliefs and activities. Each time, he was eventually released. One final time, however, in 1963, he was accused of organizing a sabotage—when protesters aim to destroy property, such as power lines, power plants, and government buildings—and trying to organize a violent revolution against the white government. These were serious charges, and if convicted of them, Nelson Mandela could have been executed. But although he and a number of other defendants were found guilty, he was not condemned to die. Instead, he was sent to prison—for life.

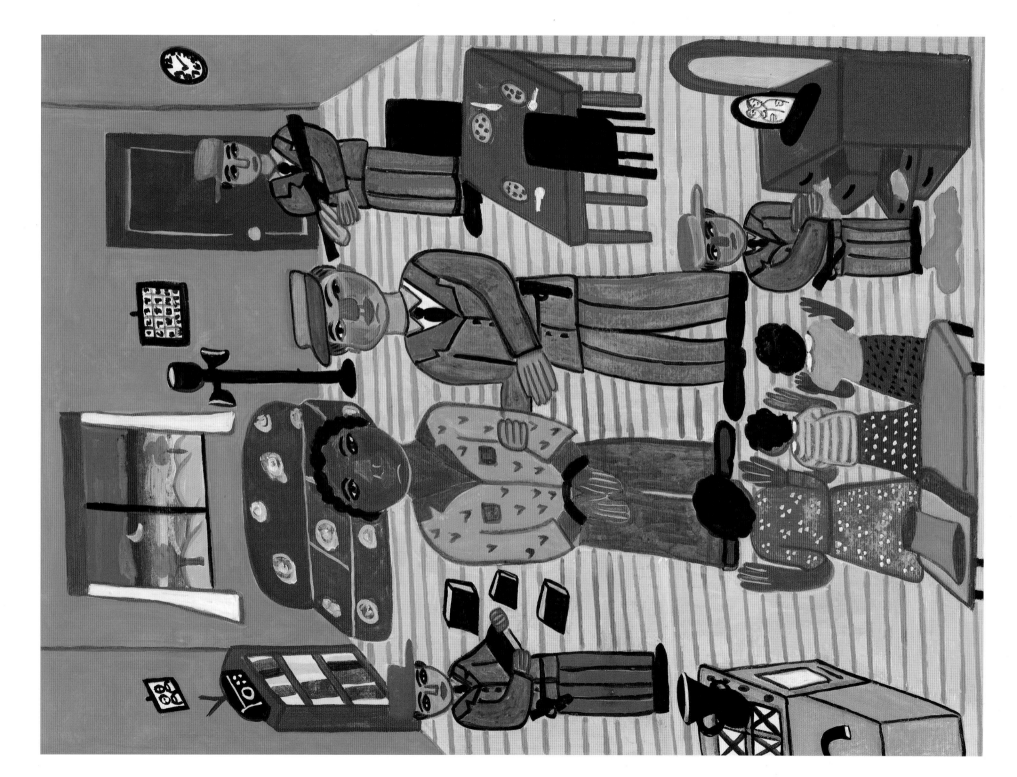

The prison, called Robben Island, was near Cape Town. Nelson was given a cell that overlooked the courtyard and had a small, eye-level window. He could walk the length of his cell in three big steps; it was so small that when he lay down, he could feel the wall with his feet and his head touched the concrete at the other side. The walls were at least two feet thick. He was forty-six years old, and a political prisoner, and that cramped space was to be his home for the next twenty-seven years.

He deeply missed his wife, Winnie, and their two children. During his imprisonment, Winnie was restricted to living in Johannesburg and placed under a curfew on nights and weekends. When she wanted to visit Robben Island, she had to ask for permission. The trip was very far—950 miles—and very expensive, so she could not afford to make it often even if she had been allowed to. Nelson could have only one visitor and receive only one letter every six months.

Life in prison was harsh. Nelson was forced to dig in a lime quarry or crush stones into gravel for hours each day. The harsh glare of the sun bouncing off the rocks would do serious damage to his eyes, because it took three years for his request for sunglasses to be granted. There were no clocks or watches allowed in Robben Island. If they wanted to know the time, prisoners had to rely on whistle blasts and shouts of the wardens.

Although the guards and prison officials tried their best to break Nelson's spirit, they couldn't do it. Even in prison, he continued to work toward his goal of freedom for South Africa's blacks. He protested the unfair prison regulations—the rotten food given to the inmates, the humiliating short pants they were required to wear because they were not considered to be men—and he became a source of strength for the other prisoners. As a free man, he had been a leader and a leader he remained, even while behind bars.

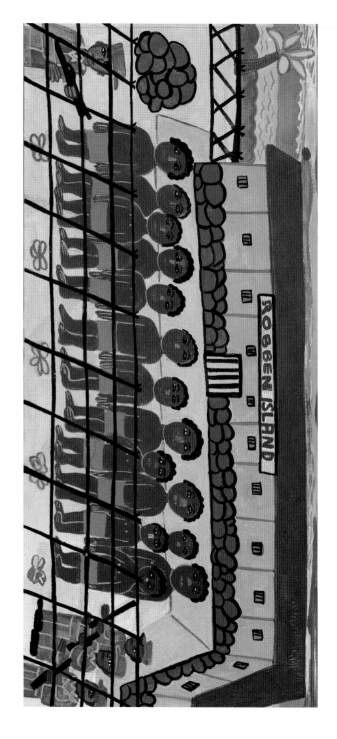

Despite being in prison, Nelson Mandela continued to make his mark upon his country. The few visitors he had were amazed by his courage, his wisdom, and his resolve. They talked about him; recognition of his name and his struggle began to spread throughout South Africa and the world. Governments, political parties, international organizations, and ordinary citizens began demanding his release.

The government realized that keeping Mandela prisoner was no longer such a good idea. Several times they approached him quietly and offered him his freedom in exchange for his promise to leave the country. Each time he refused. He would have his freedom on his own terms, or not at all.

By now, apartheid itself was under attack from both within the country and outside it. There were constant protests and violent outbreaks among South Africans. Other countries imposed economic sanctions against South Africa, refusing to buy its products or sell any of their own to the embattled country. Apartheid was crumbling.

Eventually, the South African government felt it had no choice but to let Nelson go. The country's newly elected president, Frederik Willem de Klerk, granted Nelson Mandela an unconditional release in 1990.

After twenty-seven long and bitter years, Nelson Mandela was a free man. On that glorious day, he repeated the words he had spoken at his trial years before: "I have cherished the ideal of a democratic and free society in which all persons live together in harmony and with equal opportunity. It is an ideal which I hope to live for and achieve. But, if need be, it is an ideal for which I am prepared to die."

He wanted to show the government and his people that he had emerged unbowed and unbroken by his long years in prison, and he urged them to continue the work that urgently needed doing in their country: creating true equality between blacks and whites.

After his release, Nelson was awarded the Nobel Peace Prize, along with South African president F. W. de Klerk, for their efforts to bring blacks and whites together. In 1994 the country held its first free election in which South Africans of every race were finally allowed to vote. They elected Nelson Mandela president of the newly democratic nation, making him South Africa's first elected black leader. Many white South Africans feared that he would view them as enemies, but this was not the case. He did not wish to exile them from their country, or make them experience the pain and humiliation that had been thrust upon blacks. Instead, he sought a truly democratic ideal, where men, women, and children of any race could live together in harmony and peace.

When he retired from public office in 1999, he returned to his boyhood home of Qunu. Looking back at his past he wrote, "I have walked that long road to freedom." With great courage and conviction, he held out his hand to thousands of his countrymen—black and white alike—asking them to come along.

CHRONOLOGY

July 18, 1918	Born in Mvezo, a village in South Africa
c. 1919–1920	Family moved to Qunu
1927	Arrived in Mqekezweni, "The Great Place"
1934	Participated in manhood ceremony
1938	Entered Fort Hare College, in the municipality of Alice
1940	Expelled from Fort Hare
1941	Arrived in Johannesburg
1943	Joined the African National Congress (ANC)
1944	Helped found the ANC Youth League; married Evelyn Mase, with whom he had three children
1953	Opened first black law firm in South Africa with Oliver Tambo
1956	Arrested and charged (along with 156 people) with high treason
1957	Nelson and Evelyn Mandela are divorced
1958	Married Winnie Nomzamo Madikizela, with whom he had two children
1960	Sharpeville massacre
1963	Accused of sabotage; sentenced to life imprisonment
1990	Released from prison
1991	Became ANC president and national executive committee member
1993	Received the Nobel Peace Prize, along with South Africa's then president, F. W. de Klerk
1994	Elected president of South Africa
1996	Winnie and Nelson Mandela are divorced
1999	Retired from public life

BIBLIOGRAPHY

Benson, Mary. *Nelson Mandela: The Man and the Movement.* New York: W.W. Norton & Company, 1984.

Cooper, Floyd. *Mandela: From the Life of the South African Statesman,* New York: Penguin, 1996.

Denenberg, Barry. *Nelson Mandela, "No Easy Walk to Freedom,"* New York: Scholastic, 1991.

Mandela, Nelson. *Long Walk to Freedom: The Autobiography of Nelson Mandela.* Boston: Little, Brown and Company, 1994.

Mandela, Nelson. *Mandela: An Illustrated Autobiography.* Boston: Little, Brown and Company, 1994.

Meer, Fatima. *Higher than Hope: The Authorized Biography of Nelson Mandela.* New York: Harper & Row, 1990.

Pogrund, Benjamin. *Nelson Mandela: Strength and Spirit of a Free South Africa.* Milwaukee: Gareth Stevens Publishing, 1991.

Sampson, Anthony. *Mandela: The Authorized Biography.* New York: Random House, 1999.

PRONUNCIATION GUIDE

apartheid—ah-PAR-tide

Buti—BOO-tee

icekwa—IK-kwah

kraal—KRAWL

Madikizela—mah-DEE-kee-zay-lah

Makaziwe—mah-KA-ZEE-way

Makgatho—mah-KHAH-too

Mbashe—muh-BAH-shay

Mphakanyiswa—muh-pah-kah-NEE-swa

Mqekezweni—muh-kay-KAH-zwee-nee

Mvezo—muh-VAY-zoh

ndize—n-DEE-zay

Qunu—KOO-noo

Thembu—TEM-boo

Thembekile—tem-beh-KEE-lee

thinti—TIN-tee

ROBBEN ISLAND

NORTHERN CAPE

KALAHARI

CAPETOWN

WESTERN CAPE

ENGCO...
CLAR...

QU...
MOEKE...

NORTH...
PRO...